SEASONS

SUMMER

Stephanie Turnbull

An Appleseed Editions book

First published in 2014 by Franklin Watts
338 Euston Road, London NW1 3BH

© 2012 Appleseed Editions

Created by Appleseed Editions Ltd,
Well House, Friars Hill, Guestling,
East Sussex TN35 4ET

Designed by Hel James
Edited by Mary-Jane Wilkins

A CIP record for this book is available from the
British Library

ISBN 978 1 4451 3154 2

Dewey Classification: 508.2

Photo acknowledgements
t = top, b = bottom, l = left, r = right, c = centre
page 1 iStockphoto/Thinkstock; 3 Vaclav Volrab/
Shutterstock; 5 Ingram Publishing/Thinkstock;
6 David De Lossy/Thinkstock; 7 iStockphoto/
Thinkstock; 8-9 Sunny Forest/Shutterstock;
10 thomas eder/Shutterstock; 11 Hemera
Technologies/Thinkstock; 12 LilKar/Shutterstock;
13, 14 and 15 iStockphoto/Thinkstock;
16l Medioimages/Photodisc/Thinkstock,
c and r iStockphoto/Thinkstock; 18t iStockphoto/
Thinkstock, b chris2766/Shutterstock;
19t Jacob Hamblin/Shutterstock, b Elena Butinova/
Shutterstock; 20 Creatas Images/Thinkstock;
21 Vakhrushev Pavel/Shutterstock; 22-23 kavram/
Shutterstock; 23r Image Source/Thinkstock
Cover Hung Chung Chih/Shutterstock

Printed in China

Franklin Watts is a division of Hachette Children's
Books, an Hachette UK company
www.hachette.co.uk

Contents

It's summer!

A shiny, spotted
ladybird hunts
for tasty insects.

Light and bright

Our summer months are June, July and August.

The sun rises early in the morning and sets late every evening. This makes the days light and warm.

Everywhere you look, things are growing!

Sunny days

Summer can be **hot!**
It's a great time to play outdoors.

Sunscreen protects your skin from the sun's rays...

... and a cold drink under a shady tree keeps you cool.

Sudden storms

Hot, sticky weather can lead to **big** thunderstorms.

The sky fills with dark clouds.

Then comes a dazzling streak
of lightning… and a deep
RRRUMMMBLE
of thunder.

Lightning is
dangerous.
Watch spectacular
storms from indoors!

Bright blooms

Leaves soak up the summer
sun to help plants grow
tall and bushy.

Fat flower buds open and
bright petals stretch wide.

Gardens and fields
are covered in colour.

Buzz, buzz

Busy insects flit from flower to flower, drinking the sugary juice inside called nectar.

Powder called pollen sticks to insects. When this brushes off on another flower, it lets the plant grow seeds.

Seeds and fruit

As summer goes on, plants grow seeds. These spread far and wide, ready to sprout into new plants.

Dandelion seeds are carried away on the breeze.

Some seeds grow into fruit. Strawberries are covered in seeds.

Active animals

Babies born in spring grow big and strong in summer.

Young birds leave their nests and learn to fly.

Young horses run
and play in the sun.

Splashing in
water keeps
animals cool!

All change!

Some animals change
completely in summer.
Wriggling tadpoles grow legs…

… and become hopping frogs.

Fat caterpillars grow a hard covering…

… and come out
as crumpled
butterflies.
Their wings
dry in
the sun.

Summer fun

Summer is a great time for funfairs, festivals, parades and other outdoor events.

Enjoy summer by having picnics, playing sports or growing beautiful flowers.

Did you know...?

When we have summer, it is winter in the southern half of the world.

Every four years, thousands of athletes take part in the summer Olympic Games.

In very hot summers, ponds and rivers may dry up.

Wearing white or light-coloured clothes helps to keep you cool.

Useful words

nectar
A sweet liquid that is made inside flowers.

pollen
Powder that plants swap with other plants to make seeds. Pollen in the air can make you sneeze!

summer
The time of year, called a season, after spring and before autumn.

sunscreen
A cream that protects your skin from burning when you are in the sun.

Index